A DIETER'S
LITTLE INSTRUCTION BOOK

A DIETER'S
LITTLE INSTRUCTION BOOK

JASMINE BIRTLES

B☐XTREE

First published in Great Britain in 1996 by
Boxtree Limited, Broadwall house, 21 Broadwall, London SE1 9PL.

Copyright © Jasmine Birtles

10 9 8 7 6 5 4 3 2 1

ISBN: 0 7522 2238 4

Cover design: Shoot That Tiger!
Page design: Nigel Davies

Printed and bound in the United Kingdom by Redwood Books, Trowbridge, Wiltshire.

A CIP catalogue entry for this book is available from the British Library.

FOREWORD

'Oh come on, you don't need to diet!' No really, you don't!
If you want to look thin, just hang around with fat people,
or eat so much garlic that from where they're standing your
friends will think you look thin. Dieting is for mugs – which
is just what the diet-food manufacturers are hoping you are.
So don't. And remember, don't starve yourself to death just
so that you can live a little longer.

Don't be taken in –
a banana is a chocolate bar disguised as a fruit.

• • •

Fat is a fatuous issue.

Eat, drink and be merry,
for tomorrow we diet!

• • •

Get rid of 200 pounds of ugly fat in a day.
Divorce him.

The Cambridge diet works
by giving foods such difficult names
you can't even pronounce them,
let alone eat them.

Don't go on a 28-day diet.
All you lose is four weeks.

• • •

Try the Skip diet – you skip breakfast,
you skip lunch, you skip tea…

Be disciplined –
don't eat between snacks.

• • •

You know you need to diet if you
tighten your belt and grow two inches taller.

It's not until you go on a diet
that you realise what a bad loser you are.

• • •

It's not the hours you spend at the table that add
on the pounds, it's the seconds you have.

If it tastes good,
spit it out.

• • •

You know you need to lose weight
if it takes you two trips to
go through a revolving door.

A diet that works:
eat as much as you like, just don't swallow it.

• • •

Whatever diet you're on
you can usually eat as much as you like
of anything you don't like.

If it's green and tastes like water,
it's slimming food.

• • •

Advice from Miss Piggy –
never eat more than you can lift.

You're not fat –
you're just short for your weight.

• • •

Always eat a balanced diet –
a bacon sandwich in each hand.

Don't bother exercising,
let your motto be: No pain, no pain.

• • •

The hardest part of any diet isn't
watching what you eat,
it's watching what everyone else is eating.

The best thing that can be said about dieting
is that it sharpens your appetite.

• • •

Advice if you're thin: don't eat fast.
Advice if you're fat: don't eat… fast.

Diet-food companies
say you'll be amazed
how many pounds you can lose
with their products.
They mean pound coins.

If you use a diet arranged by a doctor
she'll give you pills and a diet sheet,
and a month later
she'll expect half of you
to come back for a check-up.

Scientists have just come up with a cure for cellulite – blinding every man on the planet.

• • •

If your diet's making you lose four pounds a week, by the end of the year you'll be gone completely.

Starve yourself to death so that
you can live a little longer.

• • •

Once on the lips,
for ever on the hips.

Diet writers live off
the fat of the land.

• • •

Diets are for people who are
thick and tired of it.

The best thing to eat if
you are on a diet is less.

• • •

Picture of desperation:
a man who shaves before getting on
the bathroom scales.

Try the vodka diet –
you're so drunk you can't find the fridge.

• • •

The most slimming exercise is
to put your hands on the table edge
and push yourself away.

An exercise for the very lazy:
jump to conclusions.

• • •

You know it's time to go on a diet
when you get out of breath
going down the stairs.

One good thing to be said about diets
is that they help you gain weight more slowly.

• • •

It's time to lose weight when you have
to put your full-length mirror sideways.

You know your diet's not working if
the only thing that's thinning is your hair.

• • •

I think,
therefore I eat.

Definition of health food:
the food they serve in hell.

• • •

Diets: you can't eat what you like
and you don't like what you eat.

You know you're trying to lose weight
if you order double sausage and chips,
a black forest gateaux,
extra mayo, a Mars bar
and a Diet Coke.

If he says he hasn't had a bite in weeks,
lean over and bite him.

• • •

The first week of a diet is always the worst.
After that it's easier because
by the second week you're off it.

You can tell you're in a dieter's house
if the mice bring their own food.

• • •

If you're dieting don't just
throw out the leftovers,
throw out the originals too.

Jogging's great,
except for the bit after you put on your trainers.

• • •

Exercise can add years to your life.
Do it for a week and you feel years older.

Exercise every day –
you'll die healthier.

• • •

If God had meant us to touch our toes
He would have put them on our thighs.

Men have beer-guts so that
they can watch their weight.

• • •

Walking is only a pleasure when
you can afford to drive if you want to.

There are six million fat people in the UK,
in round figures.

• • •

You know it's time to go on a diet if you
have to pay excess baggage on your own body.

Thirteen is an unlucky number –
if it's your bust measurement.

• • •

You must stop dieting if,
when you wear a little black dress,
you look like a rolled-up umbrella.

A waist is a stupid thing
to mind.

• • •

You know the diet's worked too well
if you have to keep jumping
around in the shower to get wet.

Lose weight fast –
go on a food-free diet.

• • •

Why exercise?
Hampsters do it all the time and
look at the shape they're in!

Beauty
is an inside job.

• • •

Try the Chinese diet –
you can order any food you like but
you can only use one chopstick.

You need to lose weight if
your buttocks have different postcodes.

• • •

Don't try the hip and thigh diet –
hips and thighs taste terrible.

Don't bother eating chocolate.
Just apply it directly to your thighs.

• • •

If you can pinch an inch…
why not just do over a jeweller's.

If you can hold a pencil
under your breast you need a bra.
If you can hold a whole pencil case
you need liposuction.

You know you need to
lose weight when
your bath starts getting
stretchmarks.

Inside every thin person is
a fat person feeling really squashed.

• • •

It's time to diet if you are not allowed
on lifts unless they're going down.

You need to lose weight if you are
the same height sitting down as standing up.

• • •

It's time to diet if, when you take
your belt off, your feet disappear.

You are overeating if your teeth drop out –
from exhaustion.

• • •

You need to lose weight if you go
to your local boutique and the only thing
that fits you is the cubicle curtain.

If you can put your trousers on
over your head, you're too thin.

• • •

You have a problem if you can
eat an entire cake by yourself –
while it's baking.

People who say they
eat like birds mean that
when they're hungry enough they'll
swoop down and devour
an entire pig.

Go on a garlic diet –
everyone keeps so far away
from you that from
where they're standing
you look thinner.

Try the G-Plan diet –
you spend all your money on furniture.

• • •

If you go to Weight Watchers you can
lose ten pounds immediately,
and that's just the membership fee.

It's best to be a light eater –
start eating when it's light.

•   •   •

The best way to look thin is
to go around with fat people.

For a really fat-free diet,
eat your words.

• • •

You know you're overweight if
a 'one size fits all' garment has
your name on it as one of the exceptions.

One woman's bulge
is another man's curve.

• • •

Some diet foods have
so many chemicals you can't buy them
without a prescription.

If you want to stop eating sausages,
find out how they are made.

• • •

If God had meant us to go
jogging along the roads he
would have given us indicators.

Meal-replacement drinks
are usually powder mixed with water
and taste exactly like…
powder mixed with water.

With a cottage-cheese diet
you eat your curds and weigh.

• • •

A good diet is one that
other people go on.

Don't bother with crash diets,
just spend a fortnight in Bangladesh.

• • •

Anxiety –
the great weight-loss programme.

Exercise is like
beating yourself on the head.
You think it does you good because
you feel so much better
when it stops.

Being overweight means
everything you eat goes to waist.

• • •

Don't trust women's magazines:
they have twenty pages of recipes
and five pages of diets.

You know you're overweight
if you're living beyond your seams.

• • •

Definition of dieting:
waiting for your hips to come in.

Don't believe the magazines when
they tell you the sleek will inherit the earth.

• • •

If you want food that melts in the mouth,
eat it straight from the fridge.

If you want a well-rounded life,
give up exercise.

• • •

It's easy to keep your figure...
it's just that some people keep it
buried deeper than others.

Definition of a diet book:
a word to the wides.

• • •

If you need to improve your shape
do an aerobics class –
it's a re-form school.

Definition of a hangover:
the part of the stomach that hides your belt.

• • •

The Westerner's average diet
consists of four main food groups:
fat, oil, grease and cholesterol.

If you are constantly on and off diets
you're living in the fat lane.

• • •

The original meaning of a health club
is a big stick of wood to beat the daylights
out of someone you hate.

Dieticians say we should watch what we eat.
Who eats with their eyes closed anyway?

• • •

Definition of a carnivore:
one who only eats at drive-in restaurants.

Most people have no trouble
lowering cholesterol – into their mouths.

• • •

If you really want to make an impression,
put on five stone.

All diets promise
'the shape of things to come'
while beauticians try to
keep us 'the way we were'.

Definition of a diet:
a short period of starvation
followed by a
rapid gain of five pounds.

If your diet is getting you down
try to keep your chins up.

• • •

Definition of someone
on a liquid diet: a drunk.

The posher the gym
the slimmer the wallet.

• • •

Join an aerobics class –
be a mover and shaker.

Diet religiously –
don't eat in church.

• • •

Definition of a girdle:
an accessory after the fat.

Some diets are so good
they take your breadth away.

• • •

If you shop in supermarkets,
exercise shelf control.

You know you're at a
top-notch health club
if they weigh your
wallet at the door.

Eat, drink and be merry,
so long as you don't mind
becoming a silly,
overweight alcoholic.

Keep an open mind
and a closed refrigerator.

• • •

Go on the champagne diet –
lose £100 in a day!

If you cheat on a diet
you gain in the end.

• • •

An onion a day
gives your diet away.

No one in the world has
more strength than the one
who can stop after
eating just one Pringle.

Don't dream about
marshmallows –
you may find you've
eaten your pillow.

Nothing you put in a Knickerbocker Glory
is as fattening as a spoon.

• • •

If you don't bother about your diet
everything may go to pot.

Give a mother an inch and straight away
the whole family is on a diet.

• • •

People who keep saying they'll diet tomorrow
are just wishful shrinkers.

Go to a paint shop –
you can get thinner there.

• • •

Running is a strange and unnatural act
unless its from danger or to the loo.

You know you're overweight if…
come on, you know you're overweight!

• • •

Sadly, overeating is not
a secret vice.

If you're on your own
and you can hear heavy breathing,
you're doing the
wrong kind of exercise.

Dieting breeds familiarity –
with the same six pounds
you have lost and gained
over and over again.

You know you need more exercise
if your dog's too fat.

• • •

The hardest part of dieting
is keeping your mouth shut.

There's nothing so traitorous as
bathroom scales that you can't adjust.

• • •

Remember, a fibre diet does not include
chewing your cardigan.

No one in their right mind
should want to replace a meal
with a drink that looks, tastes and feels
like coloured wallpaper paste.

Alternative healers say
the amount of cellulite we have depends
on what we were in past lives –
so most of us must have been oranges.

Funny how diets are
always about to start – tomorrow.

• • •

If you want to look thin for your lover,
get him to take his glasses off.

Things are getting out of hand if Sally Ferries
offer you a job as a plug for their rear-door cavity.

• • •

You know you're in trouble if
your weight-loss centre has a recovery room.

A Mars a day helps you
work, rest and weigh.

• • •

It's one of life's little ironies that
'cellulite' sounds like a low fat spread.

A teenage girl is a diet
waiting to happen.

• • •

A little and often doesn't mean
a tube of Smarties every five minutes.

If you want to lose weight
think of eating as a wine-tasting –
eat as much as you like
and then spit it out.

It's time to diet if
you see a colourful zeppelin
reflected in a shop window,
look round and realise it's you.

An apple a day…
is a sign of desperation.

• • •

Take Speed to lose weight and
you'll just end up eating faster.

If you are what you eat then most of us
are a large bag of chips.

• • •

If you're past the age of 16 you don't have
puppy fat you're just an old dog.

The F-plan diet –
for people who think 'E's are too soft.

• • •

You're not fat, you just have heavy bones…
carried in a stomach pouch.

If you can't manage a staple diet,
try eating paper clips.

• • •

Try the ten-pints-a-day diet –
it's what puts the 'fat' into 'father'.

The stouter person is like
a well-built classic car –
built for comfort,
not speed.

An effective
appetite suppressant:
watching a party political broadcast
before each meal.

Try the high-fibre diet –
cardboard cookies,
chipboard crackers
and as much hessian as you
can stuff in your gob.

Try the grapefruit diet –
it doesn't make you thin
but after a month your skin
takes on a lovely,
shiny yellow colour.

If you want a more favourable
version of your weight,
have it calculated by the people
who work out the Government's
unemployment figures.

Don't be depressed by your T-shirt size,
the real meanings of those labels are
S – Stunted, M – Mediocre,
L – Lovely and
XL – Extra Lovely.

In another era
aerobics instructors
would have been drafted by
the Nazi war office.

When you see the price
of low-fat food you realise
that if you want to do without,
you have to pay for it.

You know you're too thin
if Kate Moss sends you food parcels.

• • •

Only make fun of fat people who are
so overweight they can't run after you.

A quick way to look thinner –
wear clothes that are two sizes too big for you.

• • •

Hot chilli-pepper salads will
take your breadth away.

Every type of food is bad for you
in some way except watercress,
and if you eat that all the time
you'll go green.

The best use for diet books
is under a table-leg
to stop the table wobbling
while you're eating.

A glutton is someone who keeps helping himself
because he can't help himself.

• • •

Remember, liposuction does not mean
eating whatever you can suck
through a straw.

You know you're too fat
if *National Geographic*
send a photographer round
to climb your North Face.

An elephant can eat 350 pounds
of food in one day, which is
almost as much as someone
who has just given up a
six-month lettuce-leaf diet.

If the temptation to eat
a large quantity of chocolate bars
seems irresistible, there is only
one way to conquer it:
eat a large quantity of cakes instead.

If you're conscious of your size
choose a job that will
hide your bulk –
such as playing the double bass.

Make yourself look slimmer
with dark clothing –
then try to stand against dark,
shadowy backgrounds.

Always date people who
are fatter than you.

• • •

If you want to halve your weight,
use two adjacent sets of scales and
put one foot on each.

Lose pounds fast –
donate a kidney.

• • •

You know it's time to diet when
you put on a grey suit and
sailors try to board you.

If you order apple pie in a cafe
have it without cream.
If they don't have cream,
order it without custard instead.

Julius Caesar didn't like
'lean and hungry men', he wanted
men about him that were fat.
But then, he hadn't met Robert Maxwell.

You're too thin if you go to Amsterdam
and you're the only person who
doesn't get asked to smuggle 20 kilos
of drugs back in their underwear.

If you want to eat less go to cafes
where you can see the overweight,
sweaty chef with a skin problem
preparing your food.

Put yourself off your food – eat opposite
someone who talks with their mouth very full.

• • •

Eat out and lose weight:
always choose a table next to the Gents
where you can catch the aroma.

You know you're overweight if you go
out jogging and it shows up on the Richter scale.

• • •

If you want to lose weight,
always eat at hospital cafeterias next to
surgeons discussing their operations.